T0247463

Paperback edition published by Little Toller Books in 2018
Little Toller Books, Lower Dairy, Toller Fratrum, Dorset

Words © Richard Skelton 2015

Illustrations © Michael Kirkman 2015

Typeset in Caslon and Perpetua by Little Toller Books and Richard Skelton

All papers used by Little Toller Books are natural, recyclable products made
from wood grown in sustainable, well-managed forests

A catalogue record for this book is available from the British Library

Printed in India

ISBN 978-1-908213-58-7

Beyond the Fell Wall

RICHARD SKELTON

Illustrated by
Michael Kirkman

A LITTLE TOLLER **MONOGRAPH**

For Autumn

the wall is a lure
    a line cast into my waters
        it worms up the fell side and
            over into the beyond
                and I am hooked

to put down words
about this landscape
as if they were stones

to make a wall
cairn or small enclosure

the act cannot accomplish
much beyond mere ornament

cannot make clear
the occult language
of hill and meadow

but if I work patiently
laying with tact and sympathy
that which comes to hand

then at least there is nothing added
nothing stolen

and in so doing
by a subtle rearrangement of parts

a balance is maintained

a line is drawn
a marker made
to summon the attention

somewhere to rest the eyes

I.

A farmhouse. Near the old Lancashire and Cumberland border: the River Duddon to the north, a natural boundary. As was often the case, at some point, centuries ago, a new building was erected here, in the remnants of the old. Flowers planted amidst bones. There is something unsettling about living beside ruins. It reminds us, perhaps, of the brevity of the human span, and the folly of 'civilisation' in the face of enduring nature.

The Anglo-Saxons, one thousand years ago, reserved a word for the contemplation of ruin, decay, dust, and its associated melancholy: *dustsceawung*.

As I look out of the back window, I see the shattered rooms of a former dwelling. The view is a distorted mirror. It foretells my own departure, absence, oblivion. *You too will be ruined.* It predicts, with equal candour, the eventual collapse of these now-sound walls; structures which nature – as I write – is prying at, searching for weakness, for a chink in the defence.

At night the wind is always trying to find a way in, just as the bracken is always clamouring at the fell wall. Life up here, amidst elemental nature and the tumbled stones, seems more precarious, and therefore more precious. Most days we are freshly acquainted with something dead.

II.

hill cairn
marker of small rest
drawn of a subtle line of parts
act of occult enclosure

III.

The farmhouse, the byre, the barn; each is a wall folded in on itself. Ouroboros, the serpent, eating its own tail. Beginning and end indeterminable. When left to its own devices each structure returns to a wall proper, abandoning any pretence at civility. Paint peels. Windows shatter. Woodwork rots. Like the eyes of a corpse the roof is the first to go. The shell of the building, an empty socket, is left gazing blindly upwards.

The dwelling looks desolate in this state. What it loses in form it gains in pathos. The mind's eye reconstructs the edifice from memory. But the wall has simply awoken, and emerging, ragged, it shakes itself.

*

Nature, ever persistent, when unchecked, reclaims: mosses, lichens, dandelions, foxgloves – a new colony of inhabitants, once kept at bay by man the solitary dictator, silently invades.

In one of the abandoned rooms a hazel has taken residence. Curtailed by the meagre dimensions of its walls the tree has grown in on itself. An edict, written

in stone: *become dense, impenetrable.* And in so doing, it has presented a habitat for all manner of small things: dunnock, redstart, robin, wren, yellowhammer. The walls, too, in fissuring, have opened themselves up to birds. They have become sites of shelter, of nesting. From dissolution springs forth desire.

IV.

The wall spans both a distance and a time that are beyond me. It is imprinted on my earliest memories. It is beguiling to think, therefore, that it has always been here, so well does it seem to fit the landscape. From afar its multitude of lines appear a threading of many seams, exposing the hills' needlework. But just like the bareness of the hills themselves, they are fleeting. The hills – palynologists tell us – were once dense with trees, and they had no use for walls. Their roots fissured stone to find tenure. Their canopies sheltered wolves.

*

Before the widespread practice of wall-building, the delineation of a territory was established through a ritual known as 'beating the bounds', in which representatives of neighbouring lands would meet at their respective edges to walk them together, reconfirming their rights and resolving disputes. The line of separation was imaginary, willed into being by the walk itself, threading the needle at various landmarks: a rocky eminence, a line of trees, a crag, a streambed.

*

Links, rods, chains, furlongs: the Enclosure Acts of the eighteenth and nineteenth century saw the partitioning of many large, 'open fields' and commons. Owners of fell-side allotments attempted to 'improve' a land already laid to *waste* by centuries of human endeavour. The fell wall or dyke they erected acted as a division between the saved and the forsaken. Farmers purged the fields of a sin of stones; broke their own backs preaching their liturgy; gathered and made an example of the lost – forced them to stand, shoulder to shoulder, for eternity. They ploughed, harrowed, limed and ashed; dug drainage ditches, told the streams where to run. The grass on the *intake* side is a rich, cloistered green, compared to the muted, heathen aspect of the waste beyond.

*

The waste is a battle-ground harbouring the memory of a great defeat. It is a sea of bracken, heather, moor grass and gorse. A kind of coast or outpost, and the fell wall is a beach of sorts – accumulating detritus, things washed ashore, stranded. Sheep go there to die. Make their last confessions along its dark perimeter. It is patrolled, not by lifeguards – or priests – but by the feeders on the dead: buzzards and crows.

*

Whenever I find a sheep skull, I lodge it within the wall that was its confessor. In its new position it gazes out over the waste. Keeping watch, as shepherds were wont to do before the last wolves were slaughtered. Its vacant orbits gaze, without judgement, on the threshold of oblivion.

Watcher, what can you tell us of the waste?

Nothing flourishes long. The soil is rotting. It is a corpse covering. A shedding of skins. The myriad rills are a deliquescence. The stones a powder of remains. The waste engorges in death. It revels. Dances.

I can show you where, in the desert of winter, the wind-hover fell for the last time. Can show you how flies and maggots gently prised flesh from bone. How the delicate globe of its skull, which once held the sky and six square miles of vole-earth, was, in turn, mapped and charted by beetles. Buried.

In assuming death I have witnessed countless atrocities. In the fields. By the roadside. The verges of woods. I have heard a music and it is delirious. Centuries are as seconds, seconds as centuries.

All is melody, all is dementia, all cold.

But surely it is not all death?

I will tell you this – that the bird in flight, following the line of the wall that is my greater body, glancing first this side and then that side, is a consecration, a blessing, a conferring of rights.

And along the old lanes, at the accorded time, the blue ones will rise, unfailingly, to carry the train of the green bride, again, for the renewal of her yearly vows.

But by the roadside the ash still shams death, mocking green and blue with grey pallor. And the bracken still leaves its hooks in the soil.

v.

Perversely, the wall is now a sanctuary to the last vestiges of woodland. Within its boundary, trees and shrubs can grow in safety, away from the prying mouths of sheep and deer. The sapling can, in time, become a tree.

Out on the fell side a rowan seed fell into a fissure in a rocky scar. It threw a stem upwards some three or four feet, seeking light, and, emerging, put forth leaves. I returned one day to find the leaves neatly trimmed back to the stem – clearly the work of ovine tooth and gum. Will it flourish, or even survive, in such an environment?

*

But, lest we forget, the wall is also a cage to the wood. A sapling must wait until an old tree dies and falls, leaving a portion of sky empty for it to occupy. If only the wood could grow outwards, beyond the wall's confines, expanding its horizons and reclaiming the fell side that was once its unbridled domain.

VI.

the least
landscape
made clear
with words
the subtle
drawn down
to nothing
put to rest

limestone   mudstone   sandstone

gneiss   schist   slate

basalt   dolerite   granite   rhyolite

VII.

As a child I faintly remember my parents stopping
the car by a country roadside in search of the place
– a particular section of wall, held in their conjugal
memory – where they had deposited a coin, many years
earlier. I never questioned them on the meaning of
this lay ritual, but it must have stuck with me, as years
later I left my own coin in a wall on the West Pennine
Moors, not far from the home where I had grown up.
I vaguely recollect my motivations: I wanted to mark a
transition in my life – to say goodbye to a landscape that
I was leaving behind. Back then, I did not know the full
implications of such a gesture. I might have been leaving,
but I was also leaving something of myself behind. I
had spun around that coin a slender filament, and I was
tethered: bound to that place, and bound to return.

A decade or so later, broken, I did so, spending the next
half-decade scouring the moors – not for the coin, but
perhaps for something the coin symbolised. Something
lost.

*

The wall is more than simply a line drawn between field and meadow, intake and waste. It is a repository for petitions, offerings, charms. How many of its cavities are stopped, not with fillings or heartings, but with coins and other signifiers of a strange and curious faith? How many of its miles are an extension of personhood, as much as they are an indication of land rights? How many of its discrete enclosures are private shrines, places of reverence, of intimate belief? And what of the ritual of its laying, centuries ago? How many of its stones were heaved into place with a prayer, or a curse?

*

The apotropaic device: witch bottles, animal bones, horseshoes, iron implements. All objects suffused with a supernatural aura and embedded within walls, buildings and field boundaries. To ward-off evil. To ensure good crops. Fertility. Fecundity.

In medieval England, the boundary of an enclosure was sometimes marked by lengths of ox-hide cut into narrow strips. Is it possible that the word *hide* itself, referencing a parcel of land, retains some memory of this occult practice? In 1876, the *West Cumberland Times* reported the activities of a farmer who had buried a calf alive, in sight of its mother, in order to prevent a spate of

'contagious' abortions that were happening on his farm. This was by no means an isolated incident. How much of our green and pleasant land is the site of ritual animal sacrifice? What testimonies to atrocities lie beneath each field boundary and foundation stone?

*

The wall sings, not just the songs of the living, but the unheard melodies of the dead.

VIII.

There are certain places, conjunctions of line and contour, where thoughts settle and cohere, and equally there are other places in which the same ideas come undone and fall apart. A walk through this landscape is one of argument and rebuttal, revelation and counter-revelation. Nothing can gain tenure for long.

*

The way is fixed: my walk, therefore, is itself pre-ordained. The path's ruttedness is testament to the thoughts of countless others who have preceded me. Each of them ushered along its length. Rounding its edges. Perfecting it.

Are we all simply passengers, driven onwards, slave to an impetus – a will – that is not our own?

Dare to leave the path, and lose yourself in bracken.

*

Up on the fell ridge, where the path splits, hydra-like, around numerous outcrops, hollows and scars, where there are hidden coombs and unexpected meadows, I frequently have the sensation of being ushered through a series of rooms by an unseen host. And, all the while, I have the faint inkling that there are anti-chambers, corridors and halls of which I am unaware – that despite my best efforts something continuously eludes me. This feeling could simply be an artefact of the way the crags and corries endlessly repeat themselves; so similar are they in their reconstitution of stone, bracken and moor-grass that they confound the memory, and – maze-like – refute the process of mental mapping. Nevertheless the feeling persists, and no matter how many times I visit, I can never get the measure of them. As I move from the lip of one shallow to another, it is as if I am being hurried past something incredibly important, profound, unsettling, just beyond sight, behind a locked and closed door.

And as I write this, I cannot help but find its analogue in my own mental landscape; that my thoughts constantly find traffic along safe channels – that they perpetually skirt an edge, a boundary, a truth.

IX.

All is melody, all is dementia . . .

   *

By the roadside something lies broken.

It is Brock, the early comer, whose praeter-human brain held the map of endless now – who marked the brant earth with scent-language, long before the great ancestor made teeth into consonants.

Now he lies bloodied and dead, breached six times and covered with invective:

first for Glade Haw, Brock: giver of disease
second for Lath Rigg, Brocc: rooter in the dark
third for Swinside Fell, Broc: maker of tunnels
fourth for Horse Back, Breac: the ill-scented
fifth for Great Grassoms, Broch: the unyielding
sixth for Black Combe, Brokko: little gray swine

and by roadside the ash has come into leaf despite itself.

x.

The high field has ceded to the waste. Bracken has found a way in, and the wall – once a frontier, a marker of human endeavour – has deserted its post, and, fallen from grace, it meanders aimlessly.

*

The field, like all of its kind, has a name. The walls which gave it shape have buckled and burst. They cannot bear the burden of language indefinitely. And with bracken, nettle and dock, the unpicking of an epithet begins.

*

The names of fields run like a hidden track through the collective consciousness, with only a wayward few having followed the bend of its logic.

Devil's Acre, Devil's Bed, Devil's Own. Some think that in times when appeasement of the spirits of place was deemed prudent, a corner of land was left untilled – and therefore sacred – as a propitiatory gesture. With the onset of Christianity, such local deities were heaped upon the devil. What once might have been the consequence of veneration became 'bad' land. And, of course, historically uncultivated land was therefore 'a devil' to work – teeming with stones and 'weeds', those native plants that dare to thrive without the consent of men.

Farn Breck
Bleach Field
Tarn Lands
Featherbed
Flit Furlong
Flood Acre
Footway Field
Stonehell Copse
Outrake   The Goar
Otter Holes   Forked Close
Fox Burgh   Foxcover
Yew Yaw   Fright Field
Vestry Light   Long Loont
Full Belly Dale   The Gaw
Stair Field   Bell Rope Leys
Gallow Leys   Coney Greeves
Million Roods   Green Sitches
Thin Porridge   Gutter Field
The Hagg   Cut Throat
Hailstones   Scutchen
Half Kernel   Birk Rigg
Peril Field   Kirk Hey
Hard Acre   Deadlake
Head Lands   Hell Carr
Spade Furlong   Wormland
Knees and Elbows   Helm Close
Old Ground   High Intack
Little Gastons   Hollow Ash
Deadman's Slade
Wych Ground
Horse Tyning
Hunger Field
The Intake
Iron Field
Peat Delf
Beggar Bank
Ivy Ground
Jack Meadow
Jay's Field

XI.

Inarguably, we might think, the wall is solid. A barrier. An edifice. But like all matter it is beholden to gravity, and the passage of time reveals its true liquid character. Just like the ooze of medieval glass, the wall lists, sags, bloats – lets itself go if unattended.

No line drawn, however straight, remains unwavering. All resolve ultimately weakens. Everything tends to disorder.

Entropy: all farmers seem to implicitly understand this fundamental law. Rarely are walls mended, except to be braced by an ugliness of wooden stakes, corrugated metal and wire.

*

There are miles of barbed wire stretched along the lengths of dry-stone walls. Ostensibly to deter sheep, the landscape is transformed into a vast stringed instrument in honour of J.F. Glidden, tuned to esoteric frequencies. What harmonies would result if all were sounded in unison? The wind would like to know, and shakes them, rattles them percussively, tries to steal their song. But they resolutely keep their melodies to themselves. In a landscape full of voices, the wires are conspicuously silent.

XII.

During the night, the wall has spoken. Ruptured.
Fallen. Who knows how long the forces which
precipitated this outburst had been at work. Perhaps since
the laying of the first stone, centuries ago. A thought long
harboured, festering, boiling, running the length of the
wall, to-and-fro, seeking release. But how to interpret
this primal utterance? The wall-builders have long since
disappeared.

XIII.

the wall begins again
resumes its line
of intent
projecting further
into the interior

the wall before you –
a fraction
of its true form
(blueprint, map
or dream)

XIV.

meadow stones
subtle language of rest
patiently hill-made
laying beyond ornament
drawn in balance
clear

TOWARDS A LITHICAL VOCABULARY (II)

rá   raise   ward

borran   cairn   cumel   currock

combe   drum   rigg

comb gale grane hollow hop logan scarth slack

cop cor dodd knape man penn pike scaw seat tor

cragge   hurst   scaur   knott   knowe   nab

barrow crook dent dun fell howe latter mell

Barbary Field
Lime Grassings
Bare Acre
Overthwart
Bear Shoulder
Aller Bed
Two Withens
Bedlam Pasture
Penny Moor
Beechen Clump
Mead Shott
Bellandy Bit
Worse End
Beyond the Brook
Cinder Meadow
Bone Dust Bit
Brandy Bottle
The Vernal
Bratch Ground
Sheep Brecks
Breach Meadow
Potters Croat
Briar Croft
Seavy Carr
Lammas Wood
Brock Hill
Burnt Ridding
Sepulchre
Thunder Field
Butter Dish
Narrow Field
May Plash
Cacklemackle
Cain's Piece
Rotten Lays
Barrow Field
Calf Lears
Candle Ground
Twizzle Ash

XV.

As I look out of the cottage window, past the ruins to
the fell side beyond, across the expanses of bare rock, the
brakes and screes, something steps out from the past,
assumes the stone's colour, pads quietly along the dyke-
back, forever glancing behind. In fear.

Who is this creature of the shadows?

He is *Vulpes,* the grey. A ghost now. A memory. Hunted
to extinction a century ago. Now familied with wolf, bear
and lynx, and all others who dared to have sharp-toothed
hunger.

His name is written here and there, in the landscape –
tethered to places he once haunted, now little more than
a rebuke: letters of absence.

His presence is noted, too, in old books that no-one
reads:

> Wild and shy, he avoided the haunts of men, and was
> seldom found lying up anywhere near human habitations.
> He and his kind were few in number.

In 1905 E.W. Prevost, compiling his glossary, tracked his scent in the words of others:

> At times familiarly spoken of as 'a lile blackleg'. The old indigenous fox of the wild and hill districts of Cumberland, now nearly extinct and replaced by the ordinary fox. The former differs from the latter in that he is 'larger drawn; lighter coloured; longer legged; shaped like a greyhound; never bielding.' There are said to be still a few of them left near Patterdale, Wreay, and Longtown. Natural historians are unable to give me any information concerning this breed, which has not yet been investigated. Bewick mentions its existence. 'The old greyhound breed have passed away'.

But in dying he finally disappeared beyond the reach of hounds, men and tapers. Gone to earth for the last time. Released from torment. Benked forever.

In the years since I learned about the grey's existence, I have often gone in search of him, hoping to discover his trace in a hidden scree-doup or beneath a forgotten scaur, deep within the interior. And as I stray off the paths and find myself amongst deserted borrans, bields and draw-places, I imagine his eyes looking back at me with something like reproach.

In killing me you have killed this place. It is a graveyard now, and even the yew can endure here no longer.

And although the wall offered obscurity, shelter, protection, to the grey, men bent it to their purpose, made it complicit in slaughter. They turned the stones in on themselves. Ouroboros the serpent, eating its own tale. In certain places in the Cumbrian uplands, such as the hills above Nether Wasdale, Eskdale and Ulpha, there are the remnants of these small, circular monuments. They are the vestiges of stone traps, abandoned in the nineteenth century, but once baited with flesh, to lure the grey and his kind inside, where, unable to escape, he would die.

The shadow on the fell diminishes. Becomes indistinguishable from stone.

Vulpes, do not run, as I mean no harm. I too have suffered.

*

A blood-letting is needed here – an exchange of human substance for that which was taken. A propitiatory gesture. Something to feed the soil and atone for the sins of the fathers.

XVI.

A thought from the past – the principle of reuse, its
inherent economy, is subtly present everywhere. The
building is derelict. Its bones are picked and deposited
elsewhere. Its once discrete proportions are extended,
transformed. The building does not diminish materially –
its geometries are fractured, its planes of intersection
are made more complex. All forms are temporal. Matter
may endure, but the pattern it adopts may change. Each
structure contains implicitly within it all its pasts and
futures simultaneously.

The building was once a wall, a rubble field, a rock
outcrop, sediment, magma – and will in due course
become a wall again, a glacial moraine, a lake bed.
All these possibilities are mapped within it, along the
oblique alignments and angles of each stone as it abuts
the next.

XVII.

The land inhabits, just as it is inhabited. Everything is reciprocal. Equal and opposite.

Another edict: *Enter into the landscape. Repeatedly.*
And in so doing it enters into you.

Here, in this relic Cumbrian valley, where days can drift by without human contact, the divide between the inner and outer effortlessly elides. As I roam I forget myself. The line between thought and speech blurs. Body and presence diminish or extend.

These thoughts, laid down incrementally, though my own are also the product of path, of streambed, of hedgerow. They are equally prompted by the rises and hollows of the land itself, its myriad rhythms, as they are the transits of the mind.

Some evenings, when I return to the cottage with my mind tuned to a particular word-melody, I reflect upon the fact that this could be a benign form of echolalia – that I am borrowing the words of something *other*.

But what speech patterns does this glacier-ravaged topography evidence? Just as my frequent excursions into the valley's interior have resulted in dead ends, pit-falls, precipices, so too must they result in aphasia, asyndesis, asemia. A tautology: as I assemble these words, stone by stone, I sometimes wonder – have I walled myself in?

XVIII.

The wall is language. A form of writing. A sentence. A line of thought. But how to read those hermetic marks? Granite, limestone, slate, sandstone. *Diaeresis, macron, breve, cedilla.*

buck and doe   cock and hen

cam   cap   coping   keapp   topper

fillings   hearting

jumper   through-stone

cripple hole   hare gate   hogg hole

smoot   thawl   water gate

footing   found   shiner

dyke   fence   hedge   wall

Carry Nothing
Borrow Bread
Ozier Holt
Providence
Chatter Holt
Old Blake
Cock Crow
Wheat Cake
Coldharbour
Pine Belly
Come by Chance
Blakemile   The Shoules
Maple Ing   The Craught
Baulk Field   Sour Acre
Cuckold Corner   Ox Hey
Lapwing Holm
Sheer Ash
Danes Blood
Barley Ash
Mill Stone Meadow
Greedy Guts   Dead Acres
Honey Bags   Dear Bought
Querne Acre
Devil's Acre
Fan Field
Devil's Neck
Driftway
Rack Piece
Great Drift
Snake's Tail
Dripping Pan
Scratter
Drunken Field
Dub Close
Sermon Acre
Ducking Stool
Kitching Pasture
Dust Furlong
Empty Purse

XIX.

the cairn
cannot work
cannot summon
stones to language
is stolen
clear
of words
beyond balance

XX.

All is melody . . .

    *

In the May fields, at a point equidistant, you may hear the gowk of the high wood and the gowk of the low wood call to the void.

You may hear, in their subtle variation of pitch and rhythm, an ancient plainsong sung over the distant river's burden.

    *

There is a sense, in the golden lanes before dusk, of losing. In the faded lanes at dusk of forgetting. A sense that you may take leave beneath thorn and elder, and stray beyond the verge of yourself.

A sense that the gowk call revives an old memory from within the green lanes at dusk. A sense that the cobb tree shivers in anticipation.

A scent in the dark lanes after dusk of fragrant death, as something fulvous steps out of cover, and pads along the dark lanes after dusk.

XXI.

The wall is a stoop for crows, buzzards and
sparrowhawks. Its coping is notched with guano; an
undecipherable bird-ogham. Finches, pipits and wagtails
patrol its length. They signal to each other with a
staccato call and a flick of the tail – my presence is noted,
and the message travels along the line; part morse, part
semaphore; doubly impenetrable. Before I have crossed
the first stile I have been identified as a threat. An
interloper. Nature's body is in panic-mode, and the wall
is its nervous system.

XXII.

The wall is living. Its bones are fleshed by ferns, nettles and mosses. Lichens trace it with their family trees, some so brightly coloured they appear like garish daubs of paint: a graffiti of hereditary bonds.

XXIII.

The wall is living, and lived in. It is as much composed
of cavities, tunnels and vents – of breath itself – as it is
bodied by stone. Within its recessed chambers are nests,
beyond the hand's reach. Shelters. Places of protection.
*As you pass the wall, eyes are upon you, ears are listening,
from within.*

Those gaps, those interstices, are the wall's mouths, each
with a jutting avian or mammalian tongue. *Be careful, if
you go near.*

XXIV.

Those gaps, those interstices, are not just channels for small birds and mammals, or footings for roots and stems. *They are chambers of light.*

Before dusk, when the sun is at its lowest, just as it dips below the horizon, it sends out its golden substance to be caught in the wall's net; welcomed within its deepest recesses, where it is cradled until dawn.

Thus, during the darkest reaches of the night, the wall is lit from within.

XXV.

You cannot approach this place quietly. The terrain does not permit it. Slates clatter and rupture underfoot. They invite noise, revel in cacophony. The sound of stone comes back to you, not merely as an echo, but as a voice amongst the dereliction. Men have long abandoned the mine, but others still work it. A natural industry flourishes amongst the rubble, attending to the discarded innards of mountains. This particular worker is the wheatear, sometimes known colloquially as the *stone chacker* – a creature part bird, part stone. Its vocabulary is chipped from the very slate; *clack clack clack*. In the Gaelic language the bird's name itself is onomatopoeic: *clacharan*. In one of these thousand crevices it has a nest. *Clack clack clack,* it raises the alarm.

*

Sit for a while and your threat diminishes. A brittle quiet descends. Lend your attention to the shattered wall and you will see that it *belongs*. There is a delicate hum of insects, and here and there you will observe bees coming and going from the wall's dark recesses, too small for the hand to fit.

The mass of slates piled high beyond the wall seems frozen on the point of collapse. But this is an illusion. It will continue its downward trajectory – a course of dissolution begun a century ago and more – at its own pace, and you will long be dead before it is through.

Imagine your span of years, in relation to that of the wall, as like that of a bee to your own. Think of this as you watch a train of bees leave its cavernous depths, immersed in their own unknowable, deep existence.

XXVI.

The legacy of ice is everywhere. A kind of savage remembering. This very valley is an index of its last movements – each spur and extremity a catalogue of resistance. I walk down a steep, boulder-strewn declivity towards the basin of a small hollow: a walled enclosure with views only of sky. There is release in such confinement. I feel unmoored from the greater landscape. And I drift.

We might think that such obscure places have remained virtually untouched since the ice departed, millennia ago. Only the slow blooming of lichens seems to attest to the passage of time, but another devastation has been visited here, recorded not in stone but beneath water. The sediment deposits of upland tarns are a book of pollen, revealing a story of widespread deforestation. Birch, hazel, oak, and others, once rooted soil to the fell sides, but when they were cleared the earth was gradually washed away, leaving exposed rock to which only the most obdurate life can cling: *Rhizocarpon geographicum*.

Wolf, bear, lynx, cave lion, elk and wolverine once moved through this landscape. I notice a clump of fur trapped between two ragged boulders. For a moment I entertain a wilder thought, but it is only sheep's wool.

As I make my way out of the hollow a raven silently takes up and beats a hard path through the sky, over the fell ridge and into the beyond. Those dark eyes were doubtless watching me the entire time. A comforting thought.

XXVII.

The map cannot tell you much about the wall. Its line is
uniform, neat, unchanging. The wall is variform, rough,
irregular. Perhaps, if you study the intersection of line
and contour, you can plot the path of the wall over the
hill – but can it tell you this: as the wall winds down the
fell side it diminishes in height to less than two feet,
before throwing itself off a small scar. Dashed to pieces.
But, picking itself up, it resumes its errand, following the
bend of a small, nameless rill that has cut a centuries-old,
winding path down the valley.

Likewise, can the map tell you this: the wall which hugs
the road as it descends into the next valley grows to an
immense height – in places ten feet or more, built of
stones so large that it earns the local epithet *giant's wall*.

The lines which mark these two sections of wall are the
same in character. If, then, the map cannot distinguish
between them, perhaps, at least, it can tell you this – that
they are both of the same body, and are equal in spirit.

XXVIII.

The wall shifts. Falls in. Its meaning is laid open, and, in consequence, is muddled. Time passes. Boundaries change. A line is redrawn. But that sense which was set down in the wall's first laying – is it lost, in being reassembled? Or has a deeper meaning been unveiled? A sloughing off, a disburdening of unnecessary material – a truth, once hidden amongst the dross?

Or is the wall itself simply a façade? A pretence? Did those first settlers see something written in the scattering of boulders across the field's page, and attempt to erase it, or at least, to rewrite it? Just as they made cairns to cover their dead, does the wall bury a secret?

The immovable object: rarely does the wall pass a large boulder without incorporating it into its lattice. Older beliefs and practices, too strong to be stamped out, were simply adopted. Brought into the fold. From *Imbolc* to *Candlemas; Beltane* to *May Day; Lughnasadh* to *Loaf Mass; Samhain* to *All Saints.*

Is there a glimmer, then, of something older – some remnant of profane, beautiful knowledge lodged within the wall's foundations – in those great hefts of rock, too huge to be shifted?

XXIX.

work the line
laying stones
somewhere the wall
comes down
is drawn in
made subtle
the ornament act
cannot be maintained

XXX.

The wall begins somewhere. Strays, drifts, meanders.
Mark where the wall goes and follow.

*

The making of a wall: stones added to stones.

Align yourself with them. Imagine their position as the
result of deposition. The work of an unseen river; their
direction, a tracery of its current, its objective.

Place your thoughts with them. Release them. Let them
be gradually laid to rest. With others.

XXXI.

The cottage surrounded by ruins. The bare expanses
beyond the fell wall. To what end do I cross this
threshold, leaving hearth and comfort, exchanging heat
for cold?

*

Do you not see what I have seen?

*In the field where I was laid, covered in blood and mucus,
hovering between life and death – my mother bred insensible
and unable to give suck – I had a vision of great beauty and
terror.*

*In it the question of beginnings and ends – of Ouroboros
itself – was answered. And before my buzzard-father
swooped down to take me, my pulse slowed to the stillness of
dyke-water and I saw beyond the fell wall a mass of trees. A
vast woodland, as far as eye could see. Thronged with wolves.*

*And the waste is haunted by this vision. A memory, a
promise. Its flesh is pricked by countless pollen-sores that
will not heal. Death, the wind mutters, you cannot endure
forever. They will return, and their roots will tighten around
your neck.*

Epilogue

Ice came first. Its prying, plucking fingers made combes and corries. It clawed at rock in search of something other than mountains, and, retreating in anguish, left scree-strewn slopes and rubble-fields. A wake of wall-matter, waiting to be raised.

*

The first wall-builders were the rivers. Great spills of rock. Heaved into place by the waters' many hands. Dressed with infinite care and subtlety. Mortared with silt, grit, alluvium. Coped with foam. Even the brooks, streams, rivulets – even the merest rill – could mend a line.

But restless, too. Never stationary. Stones dislodged. Knocked down. Tumbled. Endlessly reworked, transposed, uplifted. A glistening chain. The land, back then, more liquid than solid. And rivers were its architects.

*

Next came the birds, who at first were silent. At first mute. Wedded to air. Circling they heard, with desire, the ardour of the rivers' song. And in time the waters grew complacent, were content, merely, to mend, to refine – the great flood a distant memory, a myth. No more than chatter. A story to amuse the young.

And so the stones beckoned the birds down to land. Through touch they transmitted the rivers' song, which leapt into the air, leaving the waters, who railed against this theft, roaring, foaming, spitting – and in so doing spent themselves, diminished thereafter; their walls falling derelict, their song a distant, sombre refrain.

And the birds grew voices. Sang for the first time. Wherever their shadows fell on the earth, a wall erupted, rose, flourished. And the second great age of stone was ushered in upon a wing.

*

With the passing of time, the birds, too, lapsed. Content to perch here or there, to proclaim this or that furlong their territory, they fell to bickering. Their rich music, which had raised stones out of the very earth, dwindled to a mockery of its former beauty. The stonechat's 'chack chack chack', the nightingale's 'tereu tereu', the rook's 'caw'. Only the curlew's cry seemed to express something of that forgotten melody, and a sense of regret at their fall from grace.

And so the stones, untended, were quickly mossed over and forgotten; their walls became hill ridges, which in time were covered in trees.

*

Later, much later, out of the trees came strange creatures. These *men* were deaf to nature's music – to that distant refrain that held everything in balance.

These men never grew complacent when there was something to be exploited. These men never fell idle when there was time to kill. The hills rang with their industry, and so they, exclaiming with sheer effort, ushered their own song into being.

A song of work: the hills blasted open and their pores milked, their blood-ores sapped, their bones' marrow plundered and sold.

And the rivers ran, foaming, muttering, and the birds continued their bickering.

Notes

This book reflects, almost exclusively, on dry-stone walls, as evidenced in the uplands of Cumbria, UK, and so called because they contain no mortar.

The lists on pages 37, 45 and 55 are field names, gathered from *English Field Names, A Dictionary* by John Field, 1972, DAVID & CHARLES.

*

II, VI, XIV, XIX and XXIX : are assembled from the poem which prefaces the book, on pages 9 and 11.

IX : *Brock* is a dialect name for the badger (most probably a Celtic loanword) thought to originally mean 'grey'. *Brocc, Broc, Breac, Broch* and *Brokko* are antecedents in Old English and the Celtic languages. *Glade Haw, Lath Rigg, Swinside Fell, Horse Back, Great Grassoms* and *Black Combe* are hills in south-west Cumbria. The 'gray' in 'little gray swine' is a deliberate English archaism. It also references the toponym *Gray Stones*, situated on the slopes of *Black Combe*.

<u>XI</u> : J.F. Glidden was the inventor of barbed wire.

<u>XV</u> : "Wild and shy. . ." quoted from *Fox-hunting on the Lakeland Fells* by Richard Clapham, 1920, LONGMANS, GREEN AND CO. "At times familiarly..." quoted from *A Supplement to the Glossary of the Dialect of Cumberland* by E.W. Prevost, 1905, OXFORD UNIVERSITY PRESS.

<u>XVI</u> : 'A thought from the past' references the author's book, *Landings,* in which he wrote about the ruined dwellings of the West Pennine Moors.

<u>XXV</u> : 'Clacharan' – the wheatear (*Oenanthe oenanthe*), and also 'stepping stones across a river', found in *An Illustrated Gaelic-English Dictionary* by Edward Dwelly, 1967, ALEX MCCLAREN & SONS.

Some Upland Words

BRIT	British
CUMB	Cumbric
DIAL	Dialect, etymology unknown
GAEL	Gaelic
ME	Middle English
MIR	Middle Irish
OE	Old English
OF	Old French
OIR	Old Irish
ON	Old Norse
OWEL	Old Welsh
WEL	Welsh

An asterisk (*) indicates a hypothetical, reconstructed word-form.

Barrow (OE *berg, beorg* ON *berg*) a hill.

Benk a fox-hunting term, to take shelter under a crag or some other inaccessible place.

Bield (ME *belde*) a place of shelter, normally referring to animal dwellings. Found in place-names such as *Foxbield Moss*.

Borran (OE **burgaesn*) a cairn or pile of stones. Originally may have referred to a funerary cairn.

Brakes (DIAL) bracken.

Brant (ON *brantr*) steep, often applied to a path or the slope of a hill.

Brock (OE *brocc* GAEL *broc* WEL *broch*) an old name for the badger, *Meles meles*. See Notes to IX.

Buck and doe a form of *coping*. (Also called *cock and hen*).

Cairn (GAEL *carn*) a heap of stones.

Cam a kind of *coping* stone laid nearly horizontal and overlapping like slates on a roof. A wall coped in this way is said to be *cammed*.

Cap a *coping* stone.

<u>Comb</u> (BRIT *cumbā* WEL *cwm*) a valley, often rounded. (Also *combe, coomb, cumb, coom*).

<u>Combe</u> (ON *kambr* OE *camb*) a hill ridge or crest. (Also *comb, coomb*).

<u>Cop</u> (OE *copp*) a hill top or summit.

<u>Coping</u> a dry-stone wall is usually 'finished' by laying small stones, called *coping*, along its top to protect it.

<u>Cor</u> (MIR *corr*) a point or peak.

<u>Cragge</u> (probably GAEL *creag*) a rocky height, outcrop, or wall of rock. (Also *crag*).

<u>Cripple hole</u> a large hole in a wall built for the passage of animals.

<u>Crook</u> (BRIT **croucā*) a hill or mound.

<u>Cumel</u> (ON *kuml, kumbl*) a grave mound or cairn.

<u>Currock</u> (DIAL) a cairn or hill. (Also *currick*.)

<u>Dent</u> (OIR *dind*) a hill.

<u>Dodd</u> (DIAL) a small, rounded summit. (Also *dod*.)

<u>Doup</u> a bay in a lake; a recess; any extremity.

<u>Draw-place</u> a place in which sheep collect for shelter.

<u>Drum</u> (GAEL *druim* OWEL *drum*) a ridge.

<u>Dun</u> (OE *dūn* GAEL *dún*) a hill.

<u>Dyke</u> (OE *dīc*) originally a ditch, but it also came to refer to an embankment, as many man-made ditches were also accompanied by a raised perimeter. It is therefore also used, colloquially, to describe a wall.

<u>Dyke-back</u> the narrow strip of ground in a field which cannot be ploughed because of its close proximity to the dyke.

<u>Fell</u> (ON *fell, fjall*) a hill or stretch of mountainous land.

<u>Fence</u> (OF *defense*) sometimes used to describe a stone wall.

<u>Filling</u> small stones used to fill the centre cavity in a stone wall.

<u>Footing</u> a foundation stone, usually laid flat. (Also called a *found*.)

<u>Gale</u> (ON *geil*) a ravine, cleft or narrow path. (More commonly *gill*).

<u>Gowk</u> a folk-name for the cuckoo, *Cuculus canorus*.

<u>Grane</u> (ON *grein*) a small valley opening from another. (Also *grain*.)

<u>Hare gate</u> a hole in a wall sufficient for the passage of hares. (Also *rabbit smoot*). Such holes were sometimes accompanied by a trap.

<u>Hearting</u> see *filling*.

<u>Hedge</u> (OE *hecg*) a fence, living or artificial, hence sometimes used to describe a stone wall.

<u>Hogg hole</u> a *hogg* is a yearling sheep, hence – a hole for the passage of young sheep. (Also *sheep run, sheep creep*, etc.)

<u>Hollow</u> (ON *hol* OE *holh*) a depression or small valley. (Also *holr, hol, holh, hole*.)

<u>Hop</u> (OE *hop*) a blind valley.

Howe (ON *haugr*) a hill, mountain or burial mound. (Also *how*.)

Hurst (OE *hyrst*) a hillock, bank, wooded eminence or wood.

Intake (ON *inntak*) an agricultural term referring to land claimed from the *waste*, walled off and 'cultivated'. (Also *intack*.)

Jumper a stone which occupies two or more *courses* (layers) in a wall.

Keapp *coping* stones. A wall with coping stones is said to be *keapped*.

Knape (OE *cnæpp*) a summit or short sharp ascent. (Also *knap*.)

Knott (ON *knǫttr, knútr* OE *cnotta*) a small hill, craggy or rugged height. (Also *knot*.)

Knowe (OE *cnoll*) a small protuberance, a knoll. (Also *know*.)

Latter (OIR *lettir* GAEL *leitir*) a hill or slope. (Also *later*.)

Logan (GAEL *lagán*) a hollow.

Man (probably CUMB **main* cf. WEL *maen*) a rock, stone, or eminence.

Mell (WEL *moel*) a bare hill. (Also *mill*.)

Nab (ON *nabbr, nabbi*) a hill-spur, knob or promontory.

Penn (BRIT *pen*) used in hill names – a *head* or *chief*. (Also *pen*.)

Pike (OE *pīc* ON *pík*) a summit or pointed hill. (Also *peak*.)

Rá (ON *rá*) a boundary or boundary mark.

Raise (ON *hreysi*) a cairn or heap of stones.

Rigg (ON *hryggr* OE *hrycg*) a hill spine or ridge.

Scarth (ON *skarð*) a notch, cleft or mountain pass.

Scaur (ON *sker*) an escarpment, scarp or crag. (Also *scar*.)

Scaw (ON *skalli*) used to describe hills with a 'bald head'.

Scree-doup a small valley or hollow hedged in by cliffs.

Seat (ON *sæti*) a natural seat or high place.

Shiner a wall's foundation stone, but situated in an 'upright' position.

Slack (ON *slakki*) a shallow valley.

Smoot a small hole made in a wall, generally for the passage of animals.

Thawl see *smoot*.

Through-stone a large stone placed across a wall's width to 'tie' the two sides of a wall together.

Topper see *cap*.

Tor (BRIT) a peak or hill.

Ward (ON *varði*) a cairn or heap of stones.

Waste agriculturally unproductive land, generally in the uplands – and therefore with poor soil due to deforestation and environmental degradation.

Water gate a hole made in a wall for the passage of water. (Also *water smoot*.)

Wind-hover a folk-name for the kestrel, *Falco tinnunculus*.

Bibliography

Brooks, Alan & Adcock, Sean, *Dry Stone Walling, A Practical Handbook*, 2010, BRITISH TRUST FOR CONSERVATION VOLUNTEERS.

Clapham, Richard, *Fox-hunting on the Lakeland Fells*, 1920, LONGMANS, GREEN AND CO.

Dwelly, Edward, *An Illustrated Gaelic-English Dictionary*, 1967, ALEX MCCLAREN & SONS.

Evans, George Ewart, *The Pattern Under the Plough*, 2013, LITTLE TOLLER BOOKS.

Field, John, *English Field Names, A Dictionary*, 1972, DAVID & CHARLES.

Fleming, Peter, *Stone Fox Traps, Borrans and Goose Bields*, 1998, TRANSACTIONS OF THE CUMBERLAND AND WESTMORLAND ANTIQUARIAN AND ARCHAEOLOGICAL SOCIETY, VOLUME XCVII.

Pennington, Winifred, *Pollen Analyses from the Deposits of Six Upland Tarns in the Lake District*, 1964, PHILOSOPHICAL TRANSACTIONS OF THE ROYAL SOCIETY OF LONDON, VOL. 248, NO. 746.

Prevost, E.W., *A Supplement to the Glossary of the Dialect of Cumberland*, 1905, OXFORD UNIVERSITY PRESS.

Radford, E. & M.A., *An Encyclopaedia of Superstitions*, 1974, BOOK CLUB ASSOCIATES.

Rollinson, William, *A History of Man in the Lake District*, 1975, J.M. DENT & SONS LTD.

Acknowledgements

This book is dedicated to Autumn Richardson, without whose insight, help and encouragement it would not have been possible. I would also like to also thank Adrian at Little Toller, for offering me the opportunity to write this monograph, and for allowing me the scope to deviate from the beaten path.

Many thanks also to the Little Toller subscribers who have supported this publication: Tanya Bruce-Lockhart, Nima Reid, Suzanne and Anthony Kirk, Christine Shaw, Paul Jeorrett, Johnny Rath, Robert Goddard, Harriet Owens and Alex Mills, Neil Confrey, Terri White, Keith Halfacree, Richard Harms, Will Smith, Biddy Hudson, Bob Buhr, Liz Murray, Mikey Tomkins, Barbara Tollen and Howard Wix.

Little Toller Books

We publish old and new writing attuned to nature and the landscape, working with a wide range of the very best writers and artists. We pride ourselves on publishing affordable books of the highest quality. If you have enjoyed this book, you will also like exploring our other titles.

Anthology
ARBOREAL: WOODLAND WORD
CORNERSTONES: SUBTERRANEAN STORIES

Field Notes
MY HOUSE OF SKY: THE LIFE OF J.A. BAKER *Hetty Saunders*
THE TREE *John Fowles*
DEER ISLAND *Neil Ansell*
ORISON FOR A CURLEW *Horatio Clare*
LOVE, MADNESS, FISHING *Dexter Petley*
WATER AND SKY *Neil Sentance*

Nature Monographs
HERBACEOUS *Paul Evans*
ON SILBURY HILL *Adam Thorpe*
THE ASH TREE *Oliver Rackham*
MERMAIDS *Sophia Kingshill*
BLACK APPLES OF GOWER *Iain Sinclair*
BEYOND THE FELL WALL *Richard Skelton*
LIMESTONE COUNTRY *Fiona Sampson*
HAVERGEY *John Burnside*
SNOW *Marcus Sedgwick*

Nature Classics Library
THROUGH THE WOODS *H.E. Bates*
MEN AND THE FIELDS *Adrian Bell*
THE MIRROR OF THE SEA *Joseph Conrad*
ISLAND YEARS, ISLAND FARM *Frank Fraser Darling*
THE MAKING OF THE ENGLISH LANDSCAPE *W.G. Hoskins*
THE PATTERN UNDER THE PLOUGH *George Ewart Evans*
A SHEPHERD'S LIFE *W.H. Hudson*
FOUR HEDGES *Clare Leighton*
DREAM ISLAND *R.M. Lockley*
THE UNOFFICIAL COUNTRYSIDE *Richard Mabey*
RING OF BRIGHT WATER *Gavin Maxwell*
IN PURSUIT OF SPRING *Edward Thomas*
THE NATURAL HISTORY OF SELBORNE *Gilbert White*

A postcard sent to Little Toller will ensure you are put on our mailing list and amongst the first to discover our latest publications. You can also subscribe online at **littletoller.co.uk** where we publish new writing, short films and much more.

LITTLE TOLLER BOOKS
Lower Dairy, Toller Fratrum, Dorset DT2 0EL
W. littletoller.co.uk **E.** books@littletoller.co.uk